The Money Tracking Machine

THIS IS THE EASIEST MONEY TRACKING PROCESS YOU WILL EVER USE

Meyer Bendavid
Your Personal Coach

Acknowledgement

I would like to thank my lovely wife and avid golf partner, Cecile, for her love, encouragement and support; my talented son and daughter, Michael and Susan, for making me so proud to be their father; my wonderful daughter in-law Diana; and my extraordinary grandchildren, Shani, Leeza and Adam, for being such a source of delight.

About the Author

in 1987 I established myself as a licensed, <u>full-service broker</u> working with Dean Witter, Financial West Group, and National Planning Corporation. I specialized in mutual funds, stocks, bonds, annuities, life and health insurance. As a <u>money manager,</u> I was responsible for assisting my client's with purchasing securities that conformed to their risk level and helping them meet their financial goals toward retirement.

In 2003 I retired as a stock broker and decided to consolidate my business and work as an independent insurance agent. I recently published the books "The Easy Way to Tax-free Savings," "The Truth About Money," and "Craps." These books are sold worldwide.

Meyer Bendavid
meyer5757@aol.com   Web site –
http://www.thekeystosuccess.com

Table of Contents

The Facts

The information in this book is based on my ideas written on my web site many years ago.

This simple money tracking process was established because the brokerage and banking business's refused to help most of the population obtain and protect their investments.

You will never hear or read anywhere about this *simple and easy to use* money tracking process that could put the brokerage houses or banks out of business.

Everyone knows that you should <u>buy</u> stock or mutual funds <u>when prices are low</u> and <u>sell when</u> <u>prices are high</u>, but don't know how to do that.

When you hear people talking about securities it is confusing, so did you "shut off" and forget about protecting your investments from loss?

Did you lose money in the stock market?

You are probably thinking your money came back, but you actually lost three ways.

1. You lost your money
2. You lost against inflation
3. You lost the most important thing, and that is the time to get your money back.

Did you know that all it takes is <u>20 seconds a day per transaction</u> to protect your money from loss?

The following information is necessary for you to understand why you should protect your money.

<u>Divide the percentage you think the security will achieve into 72.</u> That will tell you the number of years you will have to wait to double your money.

There have been about 28 down markets since the 1930's, occurring about every 6 years. The money lost over those years could have been saved if the money tracking process was used.

Don't procrastinate. Don't fall in love with your stock or mutual funds when prices drop. Follow the rules of the money tracking process exactly to be successful in protecting your money from loss.

When you receive information from the money tracking process to do something with your money, it shouldn't take you more than <u>five minutes</u> to contact your broker or plan manager to perform the task.

If you wait, and your money is lost, lots of luck getting your money to what it was before the loss.

What would you rather have, 20 seconds per transaction tracking your money, or years trying to recoup your money form loss?

If you do not have a computer or do not know how to operate a computer, *I will use my "Money Tracking Machine Software" to protect your securities.*

A look at the past--

I can understand how you feel about ever investing in the security market where the S&P 500 was at 1441 in 2000 and now, ten years later November 14, 2010 at 1199. Why invest in something without control?

Since the 1930's there have been over 28 security markets that have lost money. Look back at the year 2000 when the S&P 500 Index was at 1441 and two years later the S&P 500 Index was at 800 showing a loss of 46%.

If you had saved $100,000 <u>without managing to protect your money from loss and you used</u> the S&P 500 Index, which generally outperforms most mutual funds in making money, your savings would have been reduced to about $55,000.

Even though there was a great recovery from 2003 through 2007, your $55,000 loss barely came back to the $100,000 and then plunged again in 2008 lower than $50,000 when the stock market fell another 50%.

If you had your savings or retirement plan under control of the <u>money tracking process</u> your $100,000 savings would have been stabilized and you would have reaped the benefits of the increase in the security market from 2003 through 2007 producing a gain to increase your savings to approximately $167,000.

As you get older, loses to your savings or retirement plan becomes more crucial. It takes a long time to recover lost money, and in the meanwhile your lifestyle could change for the worse.

Scams

In the early part the 1990's banks and brokerage houses started *hedge funding, and all types of scams and ponzi schemes. Bernie Madoff had the largest Ponzi scheme (an investment fraud that involves the payment of purported returns to existing investors from funds contributed by new investors) in the history of the United States that affected thousands of people costing billions of dollars.

In fact from 1992 to 2008 the S.E.C. eight times investigated Madoff. The agency came away with nothing and ignored a detailed letter it received in 2005 from a Boston-based investor Harry Markopoulos titled "The World's Biggest Hedge Fund Is a Fraud."

The managing director of hedge funds at Neuberger Berman stated - to protect you the following basic checks on all investments should include:

- Audited financial statements from a recognized accountant

- Independent confirmation that securities were traded at the prices claimed
- Independent custodian who holds the assets of a company to prove they actually exist
- An unbelievable amount of due diligence in the management firm before you put up any money
- Stress-testing the trading strategy and talking to the auditors

Saving money, writing checks, and handling finances are never taught in kindergarten, grade school, high school, or even college. Accounting is taught in high school and college, but <u>we learn nothing about managing your savings.</u> Shouldn't it be a priority?

Is it any wonder the United States ranks so low in savings? In fact, I found only three books on the topic; and they were directed to those in the financial business-- not the average layman.

Just look at all the mistakes in handling money that could have been eliminated if you were taught how to save without making mistakes and were taught how to manage your money to prevent loss of your savings or retirement plan.

This book will give ideas such as the money tracking process used by money managers in protecting their client's portfolios. <u>You will have the knowledge to do it yourself.</u>

The technique in handling your retirement plans are easy to understand. It would take you about <u>*20 seconds per transaction per day*</u> for a total of about <u>two hours a month to keep tabs on your funds</u>. If changes occur that are necessary to do something, such as calling the plan manager or financial consultant or broker to sell, buy or move the funds, plan on spending another 10 minutes or so for the phone calls.

Is the amount of time managing your retirement plan each month worth saving thousands of dollars?

Once you learn how easy it is to take charge of your money, teach your children.

The Money Tracking Process-

Can you spend 20 seconds per transaction each day to control and protect your money?

This system will work in any market condition- evaluating, buying, selling, Stock, mutual funds, IRAS, 401K, 403B plans, variable & fixed accounts.

For Mutual Funds or Stock-

Most saving and retirement plans 401K, 403B, IRA's, variable annuities, and variable life insurance use the security market and rely on the use of mutual funds, stock, or other securities as the underlying process for producing future profits.

Unfortunately, the process of automatically controlling the loss of your premium and future profit, provided by life insurance companies for fixed annuities and fixed life insurance, is not available for other savings or retirement plans such as, stock, mutual funds, variable annuities, variable life insurance, 401K Plans, 403B Plans, Simple IRA's, Sep IRA's, Traditional or ROTH

IRA's, and bond funds.

I suggest you follow the money tracking process that allows you better control of your savings or retirement plan. Don't rely on your broker, or retirement plan manager, if you use one, to safeguard your funds.

Recently I spent time talking to the managers at Merrill Lynch, Smith Barney, UBS, Paine Webber, and even the large banks and found those organizations <u>are not interested in protecting your money from loss,</u> but only watching your money.

They can sell stock, bonds, mutual funds; establish all types of IRA's 401k's 403B's, life insurance, annuities, etc.

If your portfolio is near $500,000 they will pursue the option of watching and controlling the buying and selling of your portfolio for a fee.

The real question is, <u>*why would I want to use their services and what makes them different from their competition?*</u>

The first process before you do any purchases of any company is to evaluate the statistical information or the flow of money by the company's sales or services.

The Evaluation Process-

It is necessary to understand the key statistics of a business.

This information can be found by using <u>YAHOO</u>. Open the <u>FINANCE</u> tag and key in <u>CHKP</u> for the quote. When the quote is shown, on the left side of the screen is a tag marked <u>STATISTICS</u>. Open this tag. Most of the information you need can be found here. Simply ask the following questions if you want to buy a security:

Is the company profitable?

Is the company's <u>equity</u> greater than the <u>debt</u>?

Does the company's <u>quarterly return</u> beat last year's quarterly returns?

Does the company offer a <u>dividend</u>? If so, it is a great option.

Is the company a leader in that particular industry?

Is the price of the stock or mutual fund greater than $5.00?

If the stock or mutual fund price is too low, the higher the risk. Keep away from the penny stocks.

Is the number of shares traded daily high enough so that if you decide to sell; the trade is done quickly?

You might look at the <u>CHART</u> and use the <u>maximum</u> option to evaluate the flow of money over the years. This might be a company for investing if the flow looks positive over a long period of time (moving upward from left to right).

(The chart is Checkpoint Software CHKP.)

Check Point Software Technologi
■ CHKP

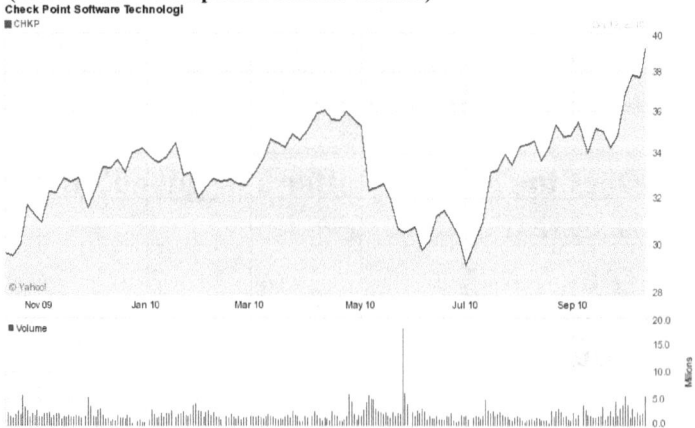

The analysts determine and project in a report the changes of a company usually by determining within five categories.

Strong buys, Buy, Hold, Sell or Strong Sell.

They may be called differently by different analysts, but the meaning is the same.

The change in category affects the price of a security either upward or downward.

Prior to publicizing the analyst's report, most purchases create an increase of the security price. Usually if the report is positive, meeting the analyst's expectations or beating the analysts' expectations in a positive manner, the security price could increase.

On occasion, if the security price exceeds expectation more than expected, the security prices may fall. This may seem illogical. The questions asked by the security purchaser could be, "are you going be able to do the same next quarter", probably not?

The biggest time of caution comes just before

the analyst's report. If the analyst's reports are <u>unfavorable</u>, you should expect a reduction in the share price. (Depending upon the analyst report, you should watch your security to determine if action should be taken quickly.)

<u>The news found in the quote sometimes will cause the security prices to drop.</u>

<u>If the company purchases another company, the prices will usually drop for fear of addition debt taken by the purchaser.</u>

<u>Foreign countries activities do affect the price of securities in the U.S. security markets.</u>

One stock I bought in March 2009 was the great American and pacific tea company – The A&P stores. The chart showed a trend that every time the security market fell the stock prices fell, and when the market changed upward, the prices rose.

The company has been around since the late 1800's. They came through many down markets and I decided to purchase it at $3.78 per share. The stock price went as high as

$13.00 and fell to a low of $2.75. The object is not to love the stock or mutual fund but to make money. I was out right after it hit the high.

Now let's get into the ideas of making money to prevent loss.

How to determine the Buying Price-

Volatility is simply the variation of the price of a stock or mutual fund from day to day or even month to month or year to year. A common way to calculate it is to take the standard deviation of the last 20 days (which is about one month of market days).

A simple way of calculating RISK --
Go to Yahoo, Finance, and HISTORICAL.

For stock- find the five most current days of trade.

Subtract from each date the low of the day from the high of the day.

Accumulate a total for the five days.

Divide the accumulated number by 5 considered an average of RISK for 1 day of trade.

In this period of high volatility in the security market, I suggest using about 2 days of RISK for the BUY option.

Use a **percent** to determine the amount you are willing to take from the highest price, as prices start to fall, and you decide to SELL or MOVE to the money market.

Example:

For buying, I will use $.50 as a one day RISK – 2 times $.50 = $1.00 and for selling – 3.5 %.

About twice each month recalculate the average daily RISK by using the method shown above.

If the average daily RISK starts to **increase** use a higher percentage for calculating the SELL option.

If the average daily RISK starts to **decrease** use a lower percentage for calculating the SELL option.

We will look at two options for buying.

How to BUY when prices drop
option one

(Use paper trading - you are not buying- just keeping a list) as the prices move downward.

Add the closed price or NAV price to (the RISK). That is now your proposed buy option.

Example: closed price or NAV price was $12.87-
buy at approximately $12.87 + $1.00 = $13.87.

The prices are still dropping:

Example: closed price or NAV price was $12.44-
buy at approximately $12.44 + $1.00 = $13.44.

The prices are still dropping:

Example: closed price or NAV price was $11.99-
buy at approximately $11.99 + $1.00 = $12.99.

The prices are starting to rise.

For the buy option -- if the prices hit the $12.99 or above that price, BUY the stock or mutual fund.

If you were paper trading and following a stock or mutual fund as the prices fall, you are fortunate to get in at the beginning. I did that with Disney and General Electric.

The question is, why use a couple of days RISK in the buy option? The answer is to bypass the thrashing of the securities and to firm up a good potential place and dollar amount when buying.

Nothing is pure and the RISK of the price falling is still there until the stock or mutual fund price obtains a good increase.

How to BUY when prices drop
option two

Another way to Buy stock or mutual funds when Prices Drop- And it requires a lot more caution, and has some disadvantages, would be at the end of each trading day recalculate the five day risk price.

Use a one (1) risk day <u>subtracted</u> from the closed price or NAV price. If you are using an online trading system use the *trade tag* and enter the *Symbol*, *BUY* option, *Quantity*, and the <u>results of your subtraction</u> for buying using the *Limit* option.

Execute the order for the next day's trade. As an example you had $10,000 to buy shares minus $10.00 for the transaction cost. You would divide $9,990 by $36.43 and get about 274 shares.

Example: closed price or NAV price = $37.42 and the risk price = $.99. The *Limit* would be $37.42 - $.99 or $36.43.

Example of the order: *Symbol* WYN, *Option* BUY, *Shares* 274, *Limit Order* $36.43.

If the stock low price hits $36.43 or lower, and the shares are bought, the advantage would be purchasing more shares at a low price. If you were to buy stock or mutual funds with option one, you would have fewer shares. The *disadvantage of option* two would be the stock or mutual fund prices drop again the following days. *If prices start to rise, quit option two and use option one.* If you did not buy the stock or mutual funds repeat option two again.

How to BUY if prices are rising

Look at the historical and use the <u>prior days closed price or NAV price</u> as your starting point. Make that the bottom price for the security and then follow the example as shown in option one.

These prices are from Checkpoint Software symbol CHKP. The dates are from September 22, 2010 through September 28, 2010.

High	Low	Difference	Closed Price
35.59	34.41	$1.18	35.51
35.12	34.12	$1.00	34.86
34.71	33.36	$1.35	34.52
34.43	33.78	$0.65	34.01
35.18	34.26	$0.92	34.30

The differences for the high and low price totaled $5.10 for five days.

$5.10 / 5 = average of $1.02.

1.25 days risk times $1.02 = $1.28 as the buy option –

If the prices hit the $34.86 + $1.28 = $36.14 or above that, BUY the security. (This is using option one.)

As of October 7, 2010 the closing price was $37.75.

If you bought the stock on October 15, 2008 the closing price was $17.43.

How to SELL if prices start to Drop-

I will use as an example 3.5% percent.

Multiply the closed price by (.035).

<u>Subtract</u> that total from the closed price.

That is now your proposed SELL option.

Example: closed price was $22.87
sell at $22.87 - $.80 = $22.07.

The prices are starting to fall.

Example: The closed price is $22.50

This price is higher than the selling price of $22.07 therefore no action should be taken to sell.

The prices are still rising:

Example: closed price was $23.01-
recalculate a new SELL at $23.01 - $.81 = $22.20.

The prices are dropping-

If the closed price or NAV price is equal to or less than the $22.20 SELL NOW.

If you still like the security, paper trade the prices as they start to drop and buy it again.

How to determine Gain verses Loss as a Percentage-

Example:

You bought 1000 shares at $10.00 per share and a transaction fee of $10.00.

The actual <u>buy price cost</u> would be 1000 * $10.00 = $10,000 + $10.00 = $10,010.

You sold 1000 shares at $15.00 per share and a transaction cost of $10.00.

The actual <u>sale price cost</u> would be 1000 * $15.00 = $15,000 - $10.00 = $14,990.

The calculation for Gain / Loss percent as an example:

Sell price - Cost price = gain/loss

$14,990 - $10,010 = $4,980 gain

$4,980 / $10,010 = 49.75% gain.

If the shares were sold at $9,500 including the sales transaction price the gain/loss would be

$9,500 - $10,010 = ($510) loss

$510/ $10,010 = (5.09%) loss.

How to Determine the Selling Price-

The Selling Prices is a calculation when the security price reaches the top and then starts to fall. This is used as a scale, for the top can be reached at different times. What you are trying to avoid is selling too early and then the security starts to trade at higher prices.

Example: The top is reached at $15.67 and start to fall.

I like using a 3.5% off the top selling price.

You use what is comfortable for you.

If the security is very volatile, you may want to use different percentages for off the top selling.

In the example: $15.65 * .035 = $0.5477. Round that to $.55.

$15.65 – $.55 = $15.10.

When the price drops equal to or lower than $15.10, the security is sold.

The idea is to not fall in love with the securities you own. The old method of buy and hold forever is gone.

The new idea is "Get in, Get up, and get off quickly." Taking control of your savings is the start of money management.

You have to take charge of your savings or retirement plans.

To be successful in protecting your money, start with the following information:

Before buying any security, check Yahoo finance, check for the security you want to evaluate, look at the statistics, charts, and latest news information about the security to determine if this security meets your risk level.

If you plan to buy securities that appear to be on a downward path, <u>don't buy the security now</u>, but use the Trailing-Down-of-Price routine, "paper trading," waiting for the buy signal when the security finally bottoms and starts to rise.

If you own the security, <u>follow the process for protecting the security as the security prices rise or fall.</u>

Check with your financial consultant or retirement plan coordinator to let them know that you are protecting your securities and will notify them when to move the money to the money market when prices start to drop, or to buy securities when you receive a buy signal.

If you "day trade" the protection system now offers more flexibility and would generate greater results.

Calculating your profit is easy. You start with the purchase price of the security subtracted from the selling price giving a profit dollar. The selling price is then divided into the profit dollar times 100 giving a profit percent.

Stock/ Mutual Fund Purchases-

I suggest to not purchasing a stock or mutual fund with a price equal to or less than $5.00 per share or stock sold on the "pink sheet." The prices may be cheap, but <u>the risk level is high</u>. The sales are usually low, and when you decide to sell, you may find it difficult finding a buyer when prices are dropping.

The money tracking process works in any market condition.

When stock or mutual fund prices are falling, I suggest *"paper trading"*(tracking on paper) waiting for the time to buy.

IRAS, 401K, 403B plans, Variable & fixed accounts-

These funds are privately held, created, or are standard mutual funds. The fund managers should supply the <u>symbol </u>of the security and the <u>name of the fund</u>.

They may have an equivalent fund similar to the one being used in the mutual fund market.

If their funds don't have a symbol or fund name found in the marketplace, ask for the web site where the daily NAV price can be obtained.

Evaluating your stock or mutual funds

an easy way of evaluating your stock or
mutual funds is to use the internet.
 Startup Yahoo and then enter the
<u>FINANCE section.</u>

For stock only-

Enter the security symbol or the name of the
company to find the security symbol.

For mutual funds only-

Under the investing tag, select mutual funds.
You can find the funds by name.
Once you reach the screen "Get Quotes
Results for" (your funds,)
under exchange, look for NAS (NASDAQ.)
Once you find the fund name and symbol,
select symbol.

For mutual funds or stock-

Once you find the price of the security, use
their <u>basic </u>or <u>interactive chart</u> as an
evaluating tool.
These charts offer many features.

You can choose a range of dates and time to evaluate the open, high, low, close or NAV for mutual funds of many trading periods.

By observing multiple time periods you now can determine if the stock or mutual fund prices are currently rising or falling. This is useful in determining what stock or mutual fund you wish to buy now or to *"paper trade"* for future buying.

There is a <u>HISTORICAL tag</u> that provides historical prices offering many date ranges. <u>This will be used</u> initially to gather the volatility of each security you are protecting.

For stock only-

Use the (5) most current dates.

 Find the total differences of <u>the high and low price</u>.

Example:

Jan 02 high $75.25 low $74.25 difference $1.00

Jan 03 high $74.95 low $72.85 difference $2.10

Jan 04 high $73.50 low $72.25 difference $1.25

Jan 05 high $74.50 low $72.50 difference $2.00

Jan 06 high $72.75 low $71.55 difference $1.20.

Total $7.55 divided by 5 giving $1.51.

Use $1.51 as the 1 day RISK.

Each stock has a different RISK level to protect your saving plans.

By evaluating these differences you will get the RISK of the stock.

Keep a daily record of the closed prices or NAV for mutual funds and the transaction date.

Getting Started-

Mutual funds are established from many security companies; therefore *it would be impossible to consider the high and low of all the securities.*

You will be using the closed price (called NAV) in the historical section calculated at the end of day processing.

The high and low price of the mutual fund is not an option and should not be used to determine future RISK of all mutual funds.

Getting volatility for mutual funds-

Use the (6) most current closed prices.
Find the total differences of the closed price.
Divide this total by 5.

Example:

Jan 02 close 75.20 Jan 03 close 73.00
difference $2.20

Jan 03 close 74.95 Jan 04 close 72.85
difference $2.10

Jan 04 close 73.50 Jan 05 close 72.50
difference $1.00

Jan 05 close 74.50 Jan 06 close 71.50
difference $3.00

Jan 06 close 72.75 Jan 07 close 71.55
difference $1.20.

Total differences $9.50 divided by 5 = $1.90.

About twice each month you should
recalculate the RISK for mutual funds by
using the above method.

Now use the same method for calculating the
buying and selling—as shown before.

Take Charge of your securities-

Now that you know what to do, call the plan managers or financial consultant to <u>move your money to the money market when prices are starting to fall,</u> or Take your money <u>from the money market to buy securities when prices are starting to rise.</u> Now you can buy more shares from the saved money to increase your portfolio.

Why protect your security from loss?

All the examples are from actual historical periods.
The snapshots are the prices from January and December of each year. More than likely the dollar values saved would be more than shown.

In evaluating what happened in the past Checkpoint Software. CHKP was calculated for 14 years for the return on an investment. With an average down market every 6 years, you would need to average 12%, using rule 72 over the years, just to break even. Your savings will take 6 years for your money to double.

The following happened if you bought 195 shares of CHKP at $22.00 per share spending $4,290 in January 1997 and held the security and didn't protect your investment from loss. (The 2010 ending date is the 22nd of November.)

The buy and hold forever method.

Year	Jan $$	Dec $$	YTD%	YTD$
1997	$21.37	$40.75	90.69%	$7,946.25
1998	$40.50	$40.13	(.09%)	$7,825.35
1999	$43.19	$97.53	125.82%	$19,018.35
2000	$109.25	$133.56	22.25%	$26,044.20
2001	$110.50	$39.89	(177.01%)	$7,778.35
2002	$40.69	$13.05	(69.98%)	$2,544.75
2003	$14.69	$17.00	15.72%	$3,315.00
2004	$18.84	$24.47	29.68%	$4,771.65
2005	$24.85	$20.06	(19.28%)	$3,991.70
2006	$20.42	$21.92	7.35%	$4,274.40
2007	$22.58	$22.26	(1.42%)	$4,340.70
2008	$21.87	$18.96	(13.31%)	$3,697.20
2009	$19.94	$34.27	78.67%	$6,682.65
2010	$34.11	$43.82	28.47%	$8,544.90

The return calculated from $8,544.90 and $4,290 was 99.19 %, and a 14 year average return of 7.09% for 14 years.

The Money Tracking Process for CHKP

By using the money tracking process in January 2001 your $24,620 for 195 shares was moved to the money market or sold.

In 2003 your $24,620 **bought** 1640 shares at $15 per share.

By 2005 your $36,080 for 1640 shares at $22 per share was **moved to the money market or sold.**

By 2009 you **bought** 1718 shares at $21 per share.

By November 22, 2010 the value per share was $43.82 with a **profit** of $75,282.76.

The buying years were 1997, 1998, 1999, 2000, 2003, 2004, 2009 and 2010.

The return calculated from $75,282.76 and $8,544.90 was 781.03% with a 14 year return of 55.79%.

The return calculated from $75,282.76 and $4,290 was 1654.84% with a 14 year return of 118.20%.

What would you rather have $8,544.90 or $75,282.76?

Let's look at Disney.

In evaluating what happened in the past Disney Corporation DIS was calculated for 14 years for the return on an investment. If you bought 100 shares of DIS in January 1997 at $69.00 per share and held the security and didn't protect your investment from loss. (The 2010 ending date is the 22nd of November.)

Buy and hold forever method for DIS

Year	Jan $$	Dec $$	YTD%	YTD$
1997	$67.37	$99.00	46.95%	$9,900
1998	$99.62	$29.87	(70.02%)	$2,987
1999	$29.56	$29.12	(1.49%)	$2,912
2000	$29.25	$28.94	(1.06%)	$2,894
2001	$27.94	$20.95	(25.02%)	$2,095
2002	$21.45	$16.04	(33.73%)	$1,604
2003	$17.26	$23.30	34.99%	$2,330
2004	$23.67	$27.88	17.79%	$2,788
2005	$27.80	$23.07	(13.78%)	$2,307
2006	$24.40	$34.27	40.45%	$3,427
2007	$34.20	$32.42	(5.20%)	$3,242
2008	$31.77	$22.48	(29.24%)	$2,248
2009	$23.92	$32.28	34.94%	$3,228

2010 $32.09 $36.95   15.22% $3,695

The return calculated from $3,695 and
$6,900 was (46.45%), and had a 14 year
average return of (3.32%) for 14 years.

By using the money tracking process in
January 1998 your $9,650 for 100 shares was
<u>moved to the money market or sold.</u>

In 2003 your $9,650 <u>bought</u> 640 shares at $15
per share.

By 2005 your $16,000 for 640 shares at $25
per share was <u>moved to the money market or
sold.</u>

In 2006 your $16,000 <u>bought</u> 666 shares at
$24 per share.

By 2007 your $21,978 for 666 shares at $33
per share was <u>moved to the money market or
sold.</u>

By 2009 you <u>bought</u> 955 shares at $23 per
share.

By November 22, 2010 the value per share
was $36.95 with a <u>profit</u> of $35,287.25.

The buying years were 1997, 2003, 2006, 2009 and 2010.

The return calculated from $35,287.25 and $3,695 was 855% with a 14 year return of 61.07%.

The return calculated from $35,287.25 and $6,900 was 411.41% with a 14 year return of 29.39%.

What would you rather have $3,695 or $35,287.25?

Let's look at Federal Realty Trust.

In evaluating what happened in the past Federal Realty Trust FRT will be calculated for 11 years for the return on an investment. The following happened if you bought 100 shares of FRT in January 2000 at $19 per share and held the security and didn't protect your investment from loss. (The 2010 ending date is the 22nd of November.)

The buy and hold forever method for FRT.

Year	Jan $$	Dec $$	YTD%	YTD$
2000	$18.81	$19.00	(1.01%)	$1,900
2001	$19.06	$23.16	21.51%	$2,316
2002	$22.93	$28.05	22.33%	$2,815
2003	$28.35	$39.13	38.02%	$3,913
2004	$38.55	$52.24	35.51%	$5,224
2005	$51.65	$60.65	17.42%	$6,065
2006	$61.63	$85.00	37.92%	$8,500
2007	$84.46	$81.15	(3.92%)	$8,115
2008	$78.87	$59.24	(24.89%)	$5,924
2009	$59.42	$69.50	16.96%	$6,950
2010	$67.03	$78.86	17.65%	$7,886

The return calculated from $7,886 and $1,900 was 315.05%, with a 11 year average return of 28.64%.

Using the money tracking process in January 2000 you had $1,900 for your 100 shares.

By 2007 your $8,200 for 100 shares at $82 per share was moved to the money market or sold.

In 2009 your $8,200 bought 132 shares at $62 per share.

By November 22, 2010 the value per share was $78.86 with a profit of $10,409.52.

The buying years were 2000, 2001, 2002, 2003, 2004, 2005, 2006, 2009 and 2010.

The return calculated for $10,409.52 and the $7.886 was 32%. The 11 year average return was 2.19%.

The return calculated for $10,409.52 and the $1,900 was 447.87%. The 11 year average return was 40.72%.

What would you rather have $7,886 or $10,409.52?

International Business Machines - IBM.

In evaluating what happened in the past International Business machines IBM was calculated for 13 years for the return on an investment. The following happened if you bought 100 shares of IBM in January 1998 at $105.62 per share and held the security and didn't protect your investment from loss. (The 2010 ending date is the 22nd of November.)

The buy and hold forever method for IBM.

Year	Jan $$	Dec $$	YTD%	YTD$
1998	$105.62	$186.75	76.81%	$18,675
1999	$183.00	$108.75	(40.57%)	$10,875
2000	$116.06	$85.00	(26.76%)	$8,500
2001	$94.62	$122.90	29.89%	$12,290
2002	$123.66	$76.26	(38.34%)	$7,626
2003	$81.65	$92.63	13.45%	$9.263
2004	$91.55	$98.30	7.37%	$9,830
2005	$97.75	$82.20	(15.91%)	$8,220
2006	$82.06	$97.15	18.39%	$9,715
2007	$97.27	$110.09	13.18%	$11,009

2008	$104.90	$83.55	(20.35%)	$8,355
2009	$87.37	$132.57	51.73%	$13,257
2010	$132.45	$145.39	9.77%	$14,539

The return calculated from $14,539 and $105.62 was 37.65% with a 13 year average return of 2.90% .

Using the money tracking process in January 1999 your $17,500 for 100 shares was moved to the money market or sold.

By 2001 your $17,500 bought 176 shares at $99 per share.

By 2002 your $20,064 for 176 shares at $114 per share was moved to the money market or sold.

By 2003 your $20,064 bought 264 shares at $76 per share.

By 2008 your $25,872 for 264 shares at $98 per share was moved to the money market or sold.

In 2009 your $25,842 bought 284 shares at $91 per share.

By November 22, 2010 the value per share was $145.39 with a <u>profit</u> of $41,290.76.

The buying years were 1998, 2001, 2003 and 2010.

The return calculated from $41,290.76 and $14,539 was 184% with a 13 year average return of 14.15%.

The return calculated from $41,290.76 and $10,562 was 290.94% with a 13 year average return of 22.38%.

What would you rather have $41,209.76 or $14,539.

Start Compounding money by using dollar cost averaging.

Let's assume you could add $100 every month to buy Disney shares. The best way would be to dollar cost monthly. What will be used is $1,200 because the chart is by the year when the money is moved to the money market or sold. The $1,200 will be added at the beginning of each year. The share price will be divided into $1,200. Fractional shares would not be used.

In 1998, 1999, 2000, 2001, 2002 and 2003 you added $7,200 to your $9,650 or $16,850 and moved to the money market.

In 2003 your $16,850 <u>bought</u> 1123 shares at $15 per share.

In 2004 your $1,200 <u>bought</u> 49 shares at $25 per share increases your shares to 1172.

In 2005 your $29,300 at $25 per share plus $1,200 equal to $30,500 was moved to the money market.

In 2006 your $30,500 plus $1,200 or $31,700

bought 1320 at $24 per share.

In 2007 your $43,560 plus $1,200 equal to $44,760 at $33 per share was moved to the money market.

In 2008 your $1,200 plus $44,750 equal to $45,950 was moved to the money market.

In 2009 your $1,200 plus $45,950 equal to $47,150 **bought** 2050 shares at $23 per share.

In 2010 your $1,200 **bought** 36 shares at $33 per share increasing your shares to 2086.

Over the 14 years you used $16,800 at $1,200 per year to increase your portfolio.

By November 22, 2010 the value per share was
$36.95 with a **profit** of $76,973.40.

The key to wealth is to **buy more shares** with money you saved when the security prices are dropping, and to compound your savings by adding money monthly.

The 20 seconds per transaction habit

Get a notebook for tracking your stocks and mutual funds.

This is an example to calculate when to sell -- $40.59 * .03 = $1.2177 rounded up to $1.22. $40.59 - $1.22 = $39.37.

On the top of the page put down the following:

This is for stock WYN Wyndham
PRICE-- DATE-- %-- SELL

PRICE	DATE	%	SELL
$40.59	1-25-2012	3	$39.37
$40.56	2-1-2012	3	$39.34
$40.37	2-2-2-12	3	$39.16
$41.48	2-3-2012	3	$40.24
$41.20	2-6-2012	3	$39.96

If the closed price on 2-3-2012 was equal to or below the highest selling price, (in this example $39.37,) you would be on your telephone calling your plan manager for your 401K plans, 403B plan, IRA etc.

Ask the plan manager to <u>move your money to the money market inside the plan</u> to protect your money from loss.

If you have an online trading system this is what you do for putting in a sell at a particular price.

Example of the sell order:

Symbol WYN, *Option* SELL, *Shares* 200, *Stop* $39.37 good till cancel.

Do not change the selling order until closed price in this example is, <u>greater than</u> $40.59.

<u>When the stock or mutual fund is not sold,</u> and when the closed price increased above $40.59, change the order as in this example:

SELL, *Shares* 200, *Stop* $40.24 good till cancel.

If your stock or mutual fund was sold or moved to the money market, you can now *start the process looking when to buy everything back with more shares.*

Without managing and protecting your savings, the following occurred-

---

In the year 2000 the Standard and Poor's 500 was $1441 and two years later dropped to $800.

$1441 minus $800 equal $641 per share lost in two years or a 46% drop in savings.

If you had $100,000 in the year 2000 and <u>didn't protect</u> your securities from loss, the value in 2002 would have been about $55,000.

By using the money tracking process to save your money, the loss was limited to about $107.57 and offered a more practical objective way of limiting your share loss by having your extra savings in the money market.

Later, you could have purchased more shares when the market hit the low of $800 and started to rise?

By allowing the share price to drop and your savings now worth $55,000 you lost four ways.

Not having the necessary money in the future to maintain your lifestyle with the possibility of "running out of money and your still alive."

There have been 28 downward type markets in the past since the 1930.

<u>This downward situation seems to occur every six years.</u>

By neglecting future downward markets you are putting your savings and retirement plans in an unstable condition.

You read about the time it takes for your money to double. When you are young, you <u>may have time</u> to recoup your loss.

Start using the money tracking process today.

It is necessary when you decide to sell or move your stock or mutual fund to the money market to use the calculations for the gain/loss of your security. The gain/loss should be bigger than your inflation level. The following information discusses how to calculate your inflation level and explain how the silent thief affects your buying power for future needs.

Inflation-- the Silent Thief-

What is inflation?

Inflation (the cost of living) compounds and is taxable. The best example would be:

A cup of coffee this year will cost you $1.00 (+) tax; next year, $1.04 (+) tax; and $1.09 (+) tax in two years.

The following is a system that allows you to compute the <u>expense of inflation</u>. Use the computed amount to calculate how much extra money you need to save over the years- - just to keep up your lifestyle.

The same system will calculate <u>the eroding buying power</u> of your savings from year-to-year.

The formula will adjust to the different tax brackets.

Most financial consultants use an average of 4 percent as the standard inflation rate, <u>without including the added-on tax.</u>

The Break-Even Factor-

The break-even against inflation <u>includes the tax</u> and is calculated for every tax bracket, increasing as taxes increase for every tax brackets.

For the 10 percent tax bracket, the break-even-percentage against inflation is 4.29 percent.

For the 15 percent tax bracket, the break-even-percentage against inflation is 4.60 percent.

For the 25 percent tax bracket, the break-even-percentage against inflation is 5.13 percent.

For the 28 percent tax bracket, the break-even-percentage against inflation is 5.80 percent.

For the 33 percent tax bracket, the break-even-percentage against inflation is 6.67 percent.

For the 35 percent tax bracket, the break-even-percentage against inflation is 7.84 percent.

Why is this break-even against inflation necessary?

As the cost of everything generally increases yearly, your savings must increase yearly just to have enough money to meet the rising cost of your new purchases.

The formula above will calculate the new inflation expense and the eroded buying power of your saving.

Inflation and Eroding-

Inflation Dollars – 10 Percent Bracket-

This example will show the extra money that would be necessary over a two-year period to buy what $1,000 will buy this year.

Year one: $1,000 savings (x) .0429 = $42.90. You would need an additional $42.90 the first year-- or a total of $1,042.90.

Year two: $1,042.90 savings (x) .0429 = $44.74 (+) $42.90. You would need an additional $87.64 the second year-- or a total of $1,087.64.

Money Erosion – 10 Percent Bracket-

This example will show how $1,000 would <u>erode over</u> a two-year period.

Year one: $1,000 (x) .0429 = $42.90. $1,000 (-) $42.90 = $957.10. Your $1,000 savings would erode by $42.90 the first year.

Year two: $1,087.64 (x) .0429 = $46.66. $957.10 (-) $46.66 = $910.44. Your savings the second year-- would erode by a total of $89.56.

Inflation Dollars – 15 percent Bracket-

This example will show the extra money that would be necessary over a two-year period to buy what $1,000 will buy this year.

Year one: $1,000 savings (x) .0460 = $46.00. You would need an additional $46.00 the first year-- or a total of $1,046.00.

Year two: $1,046.00 savings (x) .0460 = $48.12 (+) $46.00. You would need an additional $94.12 the second year-- or a total of $1,094.12.

Money Erosion – 15 Percent Bracket-

This example will show how $1,000 would erode over a two-year period.

Year one: $1,000 (x) .0460 = $46.00
 $1,000 (-) $46.00 = $954.00. Your savings would erode by $46.00 the first year.

Year two: $1,094.12 (x) .0460 = $50.33. $954.00 (-) $50.33 = $903.67. Your savings the second year-- would erode by a total of $96.33.

Inflation Dollars – 25 Percent Bracket-

This example will show the extra money that would be necessary over a two-year period to buy what $1,000 will buy this year.

Year one: $1,000 savings (x) .0513 = $51.30. You would need an additional $51.30 the first year-- or a total of 1,051.30.

Year two: $1,051.30 savings (x) .0513 =

$53.93 (+) $51.30. You would need an additional $105.23 the second year-- or a total $1,105.23.

Money Erosion – 25 Percent Bracket-

This example will show how money would erode over a two-year period.

Year one: $1,000 (x) .0513 = $51.30. $1,000 (-) $51.30 = $948.70. Your $1,000 savings would erode by $51.30 the first year.

Year two: $1,105.23 (x) .0513 = $56.70. $948.70 (-) $56.70 = $894.77. Your savings the second year-- would erode by a total of $108.00.

Inflation Dollars – 28 Percent Bracket-

This example will show the extra money that would be necessary over a two-year period to buy what $1,000 will buy this year.

Year one: $1,000 savings (x) .0580 = $58.00. You would need an additional $58.00 the first year or a total of $1,058.00.

Year two: $1,058.00 savings (x) .0580 = $61.36 (+) $58.00. You would need an additional $119.36 the second year-- or a total of $1,119.36.

Money Erosion – 28 Percent Bracket-

This example will show how money would erode over a two-year period.

Year one: $1,000 (x) .0580 = $58.00. $1,000 (-) $58.00 = $942.00. Your $1,000 savings would erode by $58.00 the first year.

Year two: $1,119.36 (x) .0580 = $64.92. $942.00 (-) $64.92 = $877.08. Your savings the second year-- would erode by a total of $122.92.

Inflation Dollars – 33 Percent Bracket-

This example will show the extra money that would be necessary over a two-year period to buy what $1,000 will buy this year.

Year one: $1,000 savings (x) .0667 = $66.70. You would need an additional $66.70 the first year or a total $1,066.70.

Year two: $1,066.70 savings (x) .0667 = $71.15 (+) $66.70. You would need an additional $137.85 the second year-- or a total of $1,137.85.

Money Erosion – 33 Percent Bracket-

This example will show how money would erode over a two-year period.

Year one: $1,000 (x) .0667 = $66.70. $1,000 (-) $66.70 = $933.30. Your $1,000 savings would erode by $66.70 the first year.

Year two: starting at $1,137.85 (x) .0667 = $75.90. $933.30 (-) $75.90 = $857.40. Your savings the second year-- would erode by a total of $142.60.

Inflation Dollars - 35 Percent Bracket-

This example will show the extra money that would be necessary over a two-year period to buy what $1,000 will buy this year.

Year one: $1,000 savings (x) .0784 = $78.40. You would need an additional $78.40 the first year or a total of $1,078.40.

Year two: $1,078.40 savings (x) .0784 = $84.55 (+) $78.40. You would need an additional $162.95 the second year-- or a total of $1,162.95.

Money Erosion – 35 Percent Bracket-

This example will show how money would erode over a two-year period.

Year one: $1,000 (x) .0784 = $78.40.
$1,000 (-) 78.40 = $921.60. Your $1,000
savings would erode by $78.40 the first year.

Year two: $1,162.95 (x) .0784 = $91.18.
$921.60 (-) $91.18 = $830.42. Your savings
the second year-- would erode by $169.58.

Eroded buying power-

As you can see, no matter what tax bracket
you're in, taxes and inflation can erode your
savings.

Therefore, it is necessary not only to increase
your savings each year by an amount that
will offset inflation you must--

That is the reason I use-- and suggest you
use-- mutual funds and stock to beat
inflation.

CD's, money market, bonds (taxable and
tax-free) -- will not beat inflation over the
years.

I am sure you will have questions. Please e-mail me at meyer5757@aol.com. In the subject area please put The Money Tracking Machine. I will be glad to respond.

Meyer Bendavid